MEET
Macaulay
Culkin

By

Sydney Cooper

kidsbooks
Incorporated

Photo Credits:

Cover: Westenberger/Liais USA

p. 6: Vinnie Zuffante/Star File
p.12: NBC/Shooting Star
p.16: Westenberger/Liais USA
p.20: Don Smetzer/Shooting Star
p.24: John Barrett/Globe Photos
p.30: Globe Photos
p.34: Craig Skinner/Globe Photos
p.36: Steve Finn/Alpha Globe Photos
p.40: Steve Schapiro/Gamma Liaison
p.42: Don Smetzer/Shooting Star
p.46: Don Smetzer/Shooting Star
p.50: John Barrett/Globe Photos
p.54: Ralph Dominguez/Globe Photos
p.56: John Barrett/Globe Photos
p.58: Vinnie Zuffante/Star File
p.62: Ron Davis/Shooting Star

Copyright © 1992 Kidsbooks, Inc.
7004 N. California Avenue
Chicago, IL 60645

ISBN: 1-56156-138-X

Manufactured in the United States of America

Table Of Contents

Introduction

His is the face that launched the biggest comedy box office hit in history. Known to millions as "the Home Alone kid," Macaulay Culkin, clapping his hands to his cheeks and yelling "Ahhh!" became the biggest little star in the world. He makes lots of money and has the kind of show biz clout others only dream about. Yet, he's only 11 years old.

What's so appealing about Macaulay that folks run to see his movies? How did he get started? Where's he going? Most importantly, what's he really like?

The first thing to know is that his friends call him "Mack." The rest of his fascinating story begins when you turn the page.

Off the set, Mack's just a regular kid.

Chapter 1:

A Family Affair

Macaulay Culkin is only 11 years old and already he's one of the biggest movie stars of all time. While it still surprises Mack that folks call him a star, being in movies is something that just came naturally. In fact, acting is like a family business for the Culkins. By becoming an actor, little Mack was simply following in his dad's footsteps—as well as those of his aunt and older brother.

Christopher Culkin, Mack's dad, grew up in New York City. His family never had much money—Chris and his three siblings all slept in the same bedroom—but they did have a love for acting in the theater. All the children were talented and all appeared in stage plays when they were quite young. Christopher, who went by the nickname "Kit" began his acting career when he was only ten. His sister, Bonnie, began even younger, as did his other siblings. Before long, the Culkin clan was well-known in New York City acting circles.

Although he was talented and devoted to drama, Kit never made it into the big time. He appeared in many plays throughout his teen years, but never got that "big break" that all actors look for. Instead, it was Kit's sister who became the star of the family. Her professional name is Bonnie Bedelia, and her most recent roles are in both *Die Hard* movies, where she played Bruce Willis's wife.

Even though Kit Culkin didn't become a star, he never lost his love for acting. As a young man, he traveled a lot and met Mack's mom, Patricia, in her hometown in North Dakota. After their marriage, the Culkins came back to New York City. There, Kit and Pat both took many odd jobs to support themselves.

Once the children started coming, Kit took a position at St. Joseph's Church, which ran an excellent private school. All the Culkin children were enrolled there.

The firstborn was a boy named Shane, who is now 16. Two years later came a girl, Dakota (14), and two years after that, Macaulay was born. Younger than Mack are Kieran (10), Christian (5), and Rory (3)—all boys. Mack also has a younger sister named Quinn, who's now eight.

In many ways, Kit Culkin raised his own kids the same way he'd been brought up. There wasn't much money, so they squeezed into a tiny apartment, and all seven kids bunked together in one room. Each child had his or her own shelf with toys and personal belongings, but privacy was one thing the Culkins rarely had. Not only was Mack never "home alone" in real life, he was never in a room alone! However, coming from such a large family, Mack never lacked for a playmate. He looks up to Shane, and loves all his brothers and sisters, but is closest with Kieran. The two used to share bunk beds and enjoyed many of the same games and toys. Of all his siblings, Mack is the most outgoing. He's the one who comes up with the ideas for things to do and places to go. Outside of his own family, Mack has always made friends easily.

Mack remembers his earliest years as happy ones. The kids played around the neighborhood, which included New York's large and beautiful Central Park—home to a great zoo—and Mack learned to skateboard and ride a two-wheel bike before his seventh birthday. Sometimes, the family would go off to visit museums. There were two within walking distance of their apartment, the Metropolitan Museum of Art, and Mack's favorite, the Museum of Natural History. Mack was fascinated by the dinosaur exhibit there and he'd beg to go back time after time to see it.

Just as **he** had been a child actor, so Kit encouraged his kids to start young. As it turned out, they didn't need much encouragement! Shane and Dakota both started with ballet lessons as toddlers. When it was Mack's turn, the three-year-old was such a nimble dancer, he got a scholarship to learn at New York's 92nd Street YMHA, a well-respected cultural center.

Even though Kit was no longer acting, he still had friends that were part of the New York theater world. And so it happened that when those friends—many of whom worked as producers, writers, stage managers, and directors —were looking for kids to fill various small parts in their plays, they turned to Kit. "They'd call and say, 'Hey, Kit, we need a three-year-old girl for this part, or a crawling baby boy for another.' Most of the time, we had one at home that fit the description," Kit remembers.

Kit and Pat's kids were happy to oblige. They all loved being on stage. In fact, Mack's very first public appearance was alongside Shane, Dakota, Kieran, and even eight-month-old Quinn. It was in a show called *Bach Babies,* which was put on during school recess for an audience of children.

By that time, however, Shane had been acting fairly steadily on his own. His most prominent performance was in a Broadway production of the play Our Town. Dakota was on her way in plays and even Kieran was being picked for parts. So it always seemed natural to Mack that every so often, instead of riding his bike after school, he went and acted in a play.

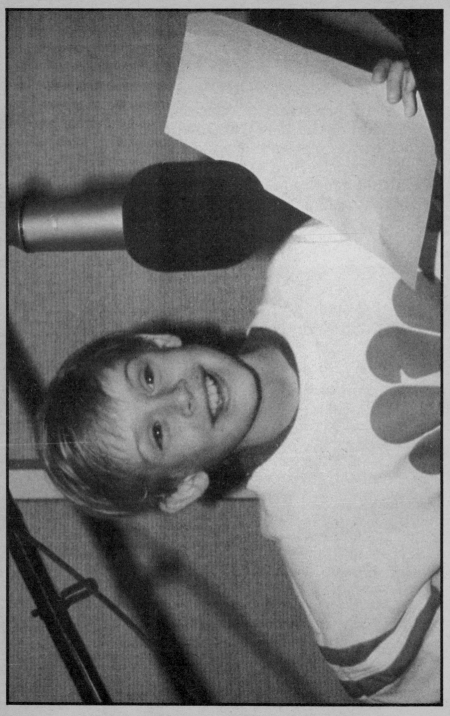

Mack rehearses for an NBC production.

Chapter 2:

Into The Movies

Most people assume that because Mack is so young, *Home Alone* was his first movie. This is not true. Not only did Mack appear in a bunch of films before that, he'd also been in stage plays, TV shows, and commercials.

At first, Mack's performances were related to dance. After studying at the 92nd Street Y, he went on to the prestigious Ballanchine School of American Ballet. There, Mack was often chosen to dance at recitals and professional productions. As a tiny dancer, he was in an operetta called The *HMS Pinafore* as well as the most famous children's ballet of all, *The Nutcracker.*

Although he was very young, Mack never felt uncomfortable being on stage in front of an audience. He also turned out to be quite a natural. While many other young dancers looked out in the audience and waved to their parents, Mack never did. He always had the concentration to stay in character. That's pretty amazing, considering he was only in kindergarten!

In 1987, a friend of the family called Kit and said, "I'm about to start casting for a new play called *Sam I Am*, and I need a boy of about six—you got one?" First-grader Mack filled the bill.

The play itself was very imaginative, but off-beat. Most audiences didn't like it much. Most critics agreed, with one big exception: they loved the little boy in the lead role— Macaulay Culkin. They called Mack "a scene stealer" and "especially delightful." Little could anyone know that just a few years later, critics and audiences all over the world would be saying just that—and many more nice things—about this talented kid.

The producers of *Sam I Am* realized what a talent they had in Mack, and quickly cast him in other plays. But Mack's parents had other ideas. They decided to sign him up with a theatrical agent and see if he could get any parts in commercials. Commercials payed more than theater and the money could help pay for things in Mack's future. As Mack's mom, Pat, recalls, "We figured we'd try and see if he could do this. That way, if it worked out, he'd have his college education paid for."

The plan worked out better than anyone could have imagined. Many commercials are cast and filmed right in New York. Auditions were but a subway ride away. Adorable, outgoing, and talented Mack aced most auditions, and landed in national commercials right away. He pitched products such as Kraft cheese, Dr. Pepper soft drinks, Apple computers, and even Gillette razors (of course, this was way before his famous shaving scene in *Home Alone*!). He also had a small part in an episode of TV's *The Equalizer.*

Making the leap from commercials into movies proved to be a snap for Mack. Of course, his earliest film roles were not starring ones, but Mack nevertheless had an uncanny knack for getting himself noticed—by producers, directors, and critics, too.

He played Burt Lancaster's oldest grandson in a bittersweet family flick called *Rocket Gibralter.* Few people saw the movie, but reviewers mentioned Mack as, "A charmer."

When Mack was eight, he appeared in two more movies. He played the son of Farrah Fawcett and Jeff Bridges in *See You In The Morning* and the ghostly son of Tim Robbins in *Jacob's Ladder.* It looked as if Mack was slowly

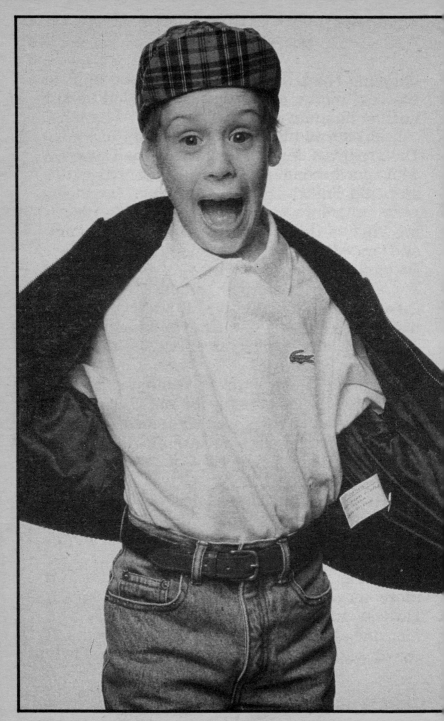

Isn't he adorable!

climbing the ladder to success—but then in his next movie, all his scenes were left on the cutting room floor!

Mack and his mom traveled all the way to Dallas, Texas, for him to act in a small role in a film that became a very big hit. It was called *Born On The Fourth Of July.* When the movie came out, Mack and his family rushed to see it, only to find that Mack's scenes had been completely edited out of the final version. That was Mack's first lesson in disappointment—show biz style.

It didn't take very long, however, for him to bounce right back into the thick of things. A very successful moviemaker named John Hughes (the man responsible for such hits as *Pretty In Pink, National Lampoon's Vacation, The Breakfast Club,* and *Ferris Bueller's Day Off,* among many others) was getting ready to cast a comedy called *Uncle Buck.* It starred comic actor John Candy as a bachelor uncle left to care for his three nieces and nephews.

As luck would have it, the director of Mack's first play, *Sam I Am* happened to be a friend of John Hughes. And when John approached him for ideas in casting the kids' roles, Mack was the first one he mentioned. Mack won the role of Miles Russell in *Uncle Buck,* and it was the movie which changed his young life.

It was more than just a role in another movie. It was a good-sized role in a hit movie.

Suddenly, Mack was being stopped in the street by people who recognized him. More importantly, Mack had won the admiration of John Hughes. And when Mr. Hughes started making his *next* movie, he made Mack its star.

That movie was called *Home Alone.*

Chapter 3:

Home Alone

One day, John Hughes was busily packing for a family vacation. He was making a mental list of all the things he didn't want to forget to pack, when a funny thought came to him. "Well, I better not forget one of my kids!" the father of three joked to himself. Then he took the thought further. "I wonder what *would* happen if I accidently left my 10-year-old home? What would he do . . . ?"

Well, of course, Mr. Hughes didn't leave any of his kids home—but he did start, that very moment, to write a movie comedy script based on that idea. It turned out to be one of his very best ideas ever.

Kevin will do anything to defend his house in *Home Alone*.

When *Home Alone* hit the movie screens, audiences all over the world howled with delight at the funny parts, were touched by the poignant scenes, and went back to see it again and again. *Home Alone* went on to become the highest-grossing comedy movie of all time, earning an astounding $500 million at the box office and video stores, worldwide.

Of course, it wasn't just the idea behind *Home Alone* that made it so amazingly popular. Much of its success was attributed to the little boy at the center of the movie—Macaulay Culkin!

The truth is that many little boys auditioned for the lead role of Kevin. Even though John Hughes knew that Mack would be perfect, director Chris Columbus felt they should look at more kids. After all, they knew right from the start that if they cast the wrong kid, the movie could easily fall apart.

Mr. Columbus has said, "I went to audition Mack first, because John Hughes thought he could do it. And Mack was very good, but I thought, 'Well, he's the first kid I've seen. How can I hire him right away?'" But after seeing 200 more boys, Mr. Columbus came back to Mack.

There's no question that starring in *Home Alone* was the toughest challenge of Mack's life. He was only nine when filming began and for the first time, he had to be away from home for months, since the movie was filmed in Chicago. Mack's parents took turns being by his side and his brother Kieran, cast in the movie as one of his cousins, was there for a while. But just like the boy in the script, Mack missed the rest of his family terribly.

Mack was in nearly every scene, which put a lot of pressure on him, especially since he had so many lines to learn.

Besides learning lines, Mack had to do schoolwork while he was filming *Home Alone.* A tutor came with him and he was required to put in several hours a day learning reading, writing, science, history, and arithmetic.

"It was very hard," Mack has admitted, "I got tired a lot."

Still, Mack managed—quite nicely—to have fun filming *Home Alone.* Between scenes, he'd set up the props to make a little playroom for himself, and engage the cast and crew in games. Mack played his favorite Nintendo games, too, when the cameras weren't rolling.

Best of all, however, was that Mack loved the script for *Home Alone.* He could really relate to Kevin's predicament, and felt that in real life, he probably would have reacted the same way.

Home Alone truly made Mack a star. He got tons of fan mail and was constantly asked for his autograph. The money he earned allowed his family to move into a bigger home. Most importantly, movie and TV offers were coming his way at an unprecedented rate. Everyone in the biz wanted Mack. He was a very hot actor indeed.

Mack bestowed his first film kiss upon the lips of actress Anna Chlumsky in *My Girl***. Offscreen they're just friends.**

Chapter 4:

My Girl

Every actor dreams of being so popular that he can pick and chose roles from hundreds of offers. Most never get that opportunity. After *Home Alone*, Mack was in a very rare, and much envied position in Hollywood. It was all the more amazing because of his age. Hotshot producers and studio heads were coming to Mack with all sorts of movie scripts—would he star in a film about *Dennis the Menace?* How about one involving a pint-sized police kid?

It was at this point that Mack's parents, Kit and Pat, made a big decision. Since they were the ones, after all, who actually read all the scripts and thought about all the offers, they decided to quit their other jobs and manage

Mack's career full time. Of course, they had some professional help from Mack's agent, as well.

With his family behind him, Mack would never have to worry about being taken advantage of, or having to accept offers that his parents might consider inappropriate for a young boy. Mack's dad has said that more than anything else, he didn't want Mack to always be typecast as "the kid from *Home Alone*." He planned on looking for new roles where Mack could play many different types of characters. And in fact, Mack's next role accomplished that goal completely.

Mack's *Home Alone* follow-up was a movie called *My Girl.* Although it had some funny lines, it was not a comedy. And although Mack had a major part in it, he was not the star. *My Girl* was the bittersweet story of a young girl's coming of age. It starred Dan Aykroyd and Jamie Lee Curtis as the adults, while newcomer Anna Chlumsky played the lead role of Vada Sultenfuss. Mack was cast as Thomas J., Vada's shy and insecure best friend. Not only was the role of Thomas J. completely different from Kevin in *Home Alone,* the character was totally different from Mack in real life.

"Thomas J. is kinda like a shy kid who's easy to ignore," explains Mack, "while I like stand out in a crowd!"

His part in *My Girl* gave Mack the chance to stretch his acting talent in a couple of other ways as well. For one thing, he got his first on-screen kiss in the movie, and for another, his character dies.

"I didn't let it get to me," he said about his most tragic scene. "I just pretended to be sleeping." But when advance word got out that the "*Home Alone* kid," beloved by millions of children all over the world, had a death scene in his new movie, people panicked. They didn't know whether they should let their kids see *My Girl,* afraid they'd think it was Mack in real life. So just before the movie opened, Mack went on TV talk shows to assure his young fans that in real life, he was just fine. "They should realize it's only a movie," was Mack's advice to the audience.

Behind the scenes at *My Girl,* there was no sense of tragedy at all. Mack and his co-stars had a ball during the three months of filming in Orlando, Florida. This time, Mack's whole family came with him and everyone got to enjoy trips to nearby Disney World, Nickelodeon, and Universal Studios. Mack himself was especially playful on the *My Girl* set.

Word leaked out about him playing tricks on his tutor, on the entire crew, and even on his adult co-stars, Dan and Jamie. In spite of his pranks, no one ever got angry with Mack, for though he was mischievous, he was never mean. Everyone felt that young Mr. Culkin was a total professional when the cameras rolled— and a total kid when they stopped.

When Mack was interviewed just before *My Girl* opened, he said he had no idea whether the movie would be a hit or not. In fact, while nothing could compare to the success of *Home Alone*, *My Girl* did extremely well at the box office and was considered to be another feather in Mack's acting cap.

Chapter 5:

Home Alone 2: Lost In New York

There was never any doubt that there would be a sequel to *Home Alone* — not only were audiences clamoring for one, but all the cast and movie people were anxious to do another as well. Mack was no exception. He liked playing Kevin and thought it would be fun to see what kind of situations the writers would come up with this time. Also, after doing *My Girl*, there was less concern about him being typecast.

Home Alone 2: Lost In New York finds Kevin's family about to embark on another vacation. The Chicagoans are headed for the warmth of Florida over the Christmas holidays. As in the original, the family includes not only

Macaulay and costars Joe Pesci and Daniel Stern filmed *Home Alone II* on the streets of Manhattan.

the five in Kevin's clan, but an aunt, uncle, and a slew of cousins as well. This time, Kevin does make it to the plane—only it's the *wrong* plane!

At crowded O'Hare airport, Kevin, following his dad, is trying hard to keep up with his group, who are rushing to make the plane. But there's a man wearing the exact same coat and scarf that Kevin's dad has—and by mistake, Kevin follows **him** and takes a wrong turn. He follows the man onto a New York bound plane. Once again, his absence isn't discovered until the rest of his family are halfway to Florida.

Kevin gets stuck in New York and finds himself wandering the streets of Manhattan. But he isn't completely alone there—by a comic twist of fate, he just happens to run into the bungling burglars from the first movie, (Joe Pesci and Daniel Stern recreate their roles), who have escaped from prison. Naturally, they recognize Kevin, and try to force him to be their accomplice as they clumsily attempt some petty crimes. Once again, it takes all of Kevin's ingenuity to get out of this new mess—and somehow find his family again.

Just as Mack anticipated, he had a great time making *Home Alone 2.* Part of the reason was that it was filmed in his own home town, New York City, a place where he could never really get lost! This allowed Mack to go to his real home every night and be with his family. There were no homesick blues this time around. Besides, his brother Kieran ended up reprising his role as cousin Fuller, working with Mack in several scenes.

During filming, Mack also got to visit some of his favorite places in New York, like the World Trade Center (two of the tallest buildings in the world), Central Park, and the famous Plaza Hotel, which were all locales used in the movie.

Mack enjoyed the special effects that were used in *Home Alone 2: Lost In New York*. Because the movie takes place in winter, but was actually filmed in the fall, the moviemakers had to make snow. Mack watched, as they used seven cannons, which shot 3000 gallons of water per minute, to create an eight inch layer of snow in Central Park.

Home Alone 2: Lost In New York is scheduled to be out around Thanksgiving and play throughout the Christmas holidays. Mack and his family are among the millions who can hardly wait to see it.

Chapter 6:

School Days

Because Mack is such a big movie star, it might be hard to imagine him sitting in a school room, being called on by the teacher to stand up and answer questions. But in real life, when he's not off on a movie location, he really does go to school, just like you do. In fact, he always has.

Mack started at St. Joseph's, the school attached to the church where his dad worked. His older brother Shane and sister Dakota were already there when he entered as a first-grader. At St. Joseph's, Mack was required to wear a uniform to school, just like all the other students. He was a good pupil and basically happy there. He had lots of friends and played after-school sports as well.

**Mack is all dressed up for
a "night out" with brother Kieran.**

Following his success in the movies, though, Mack changed schools. His family felt it would be best for him to be in a school where all the kids were professional actors. Since in New York City there are many young people working in commercials, theater, TV, and movies, there are also several excellent schools that cater to their special needs. Mack's family chose one called Professional Children's School. Along with Mack, they moved Shane, Dakota, Kieran, and Quinn over as well. It proved to be a good move for everyone.

PCS, as it's called, is equipped to prepare work for him when he goes off on movie locations. He also works with a tutor, and the school sends along lots of homework, as well. Not even a star like Mack gets out of doing homework!

He's a better than average student whose best subjects are science, math, and social studies. Mack has made many friends at his new school. He especially likes hanging out with them at lunch. He's secretly glad that he doesn't have to wear a uniform anymore, and plans on staying at PCS all through high school.

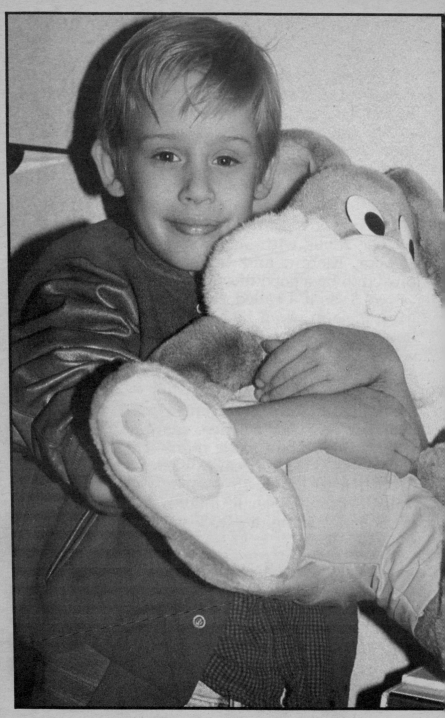

Mack gives a big hug to his favorite cuddly critter.

Chapter 7:

At Home, Alone? Not!

The Culkins no longer live in a cramped, two-bedroom apartment. Now that Mack's making big movies, and his parents are managing him, they can afford to live in more spacious quarters. They also felt they had to move because fans were finding Mack's house and starting to invade the family's privacy. Since the Culkins want Mack, and all their children, to lead the most normal lives possible, they really needed to protect their privacy.

They could have relocated to Hollywood, California, where show biz work would probably be plentiful for all the kids. But the Culkins had long ago put roots down in New York, and chose to stay there. They moved into a three-level townhouse with enough bedrooms so Mack could have one entirely to himself.

"It's a small room," Mack says agreeably, "but I like it." Still, with such a big family, Mack never finds himself home alone!

That's okay with him, though, because his brothers are still his best friends and most constant companions. After walking home from school—Mack gets out by 2:45—if he doesn't have any interviews to do, he likes to settle into a hot game of Nintendo with Shane and Kieran. The trio put their video game skills together to try and get the highest score possible. They often play on the large Nintendo Home Entertainment center that Mack got as a gift from his friend Michael Jackson, or on the hand-held Gameboy that Mack is rarely without.

In his room, Mack has a loft style bed, from which he admits to watching lots of TV shows. "I have my own TV and cable in my room. I have four pillows on my bed. Sometimes I just cover up and watch TV all day." His never-miss shows include *Family Matters, Roseanne,* and *The Simpsons.* He also tunes into Nickelodeon.

One TV show that Mack admits to not watching is the cartoon series that he used to provide the voice for, *WishKid Starring Macaulay Culkin,* a Saturday morning series on NBC. When he first went to California to record the voice for the show, he thought it was really cool having his own cartoon, but now that he's older, Mack's kind of outgrown watching cartoons. As it turns out, the show has ended its run anyway.

One show he would love to watch is prowrestling on pay-per-view. But since he's not allowed to order pay-per-view, Mack usually settles for just renting wrestling tapes.

Every once in a while, he actually gets to go to a live pro-wrestling show, or be in the audience for a show biz event like Wrestlemania. Mack has his favorite wrestling stars, including "Ultimate Warrior."

When Mack goes out, it's always with members of his family, and sometimes a few friends. Mini-golf, bowling, and billiards are favorite Saturday afternoon activities. He admits that he's not great at any of them, but he enjoys them just the same.

He still likes going to the Museum of Natural History, to see the dinosaurs and to buy neat things in the gift shop. He even once took a reporter there who was interviewing him.

As you might imagine, Mack's a major movie buff. So is his entire family. A favorite Saturday night out finds all the Culkins— except for the very youngest—sitting side-by-side in a movie theater aisle, tubs of popcorn in hand, all eyes glued to the screen. Mack tends to like comedies best on the big screen, but his recent favorites are *Boyz In the Hood,* and one called *UHF,* starring satirist Weird Al Yankovic.

Mack had a dramatic starring role in *My Girl*.

Chapter 8:

A Girlfriend For Mack?

Until recently, Mack was way too young to think about girls as anything more than just friends. Still, that didn't stop the celebrity rumor mill from grinding away. In the papers, Mack was most often paired with his *My Girl* co-star, Anna Chlumsky, no doubt because of that on-screen smooch. But it was never true that Mack and Anna had any romantic feelings for each other. In fact, depending on whose version you believed, they were either "just good friends," or "didn't much care for each other at all!"

While Mack said that he thought they related well to each other, Anna only remembered the times when off-screen, Mack would

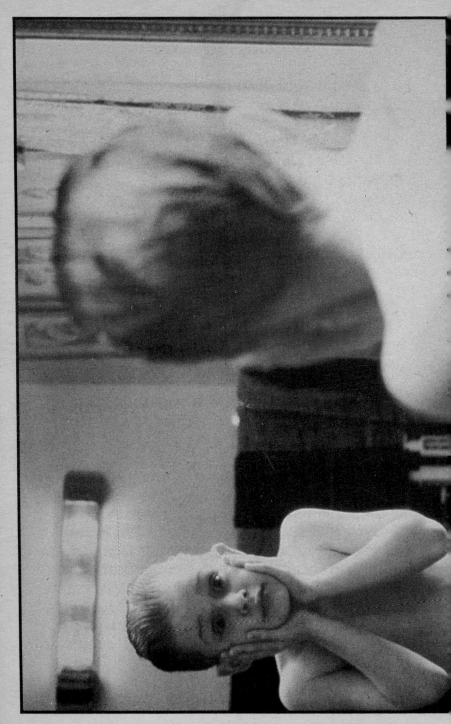

The look that made Macaulay Culkin famous!

try to get her involved in his mischief-making and goofing off. A quiet, serious girl, Anna wasn't keen on any of that at all.

Still, when Anna, who's from Chicago, visited New York for the first time, it was Mack who showed her around. He took her to the biggest toy store in the city, FAO Schwartz, and to a Broadway play called *The Secret Garden*. That's when the papers said they were boyfriend and girlfriend, but the media was mistaken.

Mack's also been "paired up" in the papers with the lovely young star of *The Secret Garden*, Daisy Eagan. Once again, however, reporters got it wrong. The talented twosome barely even know each other.

Not knowing Mack personally, however, hasn't stopped lots of girls from writing letters offering to go out with him. Some even send marriage proposals! In the beginning, Mack ignored all that stuff. The little boy had no interest in girls or dating or anything vaguely romantic. But things have started to change in that department. As Mack reported recently, "Some girls are okay, some of them aren't."

He now writes poems to a special girl at school, and is even shyly admitting that she's a "sorta" girlfriend. At first, he didn't want to tell anyone her name, and would only say, "Her initials are L.B.," but later introduced her as Laura Bundy, a blond, blue-eyed, 10-year-old actress and model. Mack had seen Laura's photo and thought she was really cool looking, so—as only-in-showbiz-tales-go, he got his agent to contact her agent, so he could ask her out. She agreed and they went to see the movie *Dances With Wolves,* and then to an ice-cream parlor for dessert.

Since both kids are busy—Laura's in a musical play called *Ruthless!,* while Mack's on-the-go with movies, interviews, and photo sessions—they don't see all that much of each other. Still, they make time to get together.

"We do things together," Mack said. "She comes to my house and I go to her house and we play video games. It's fun." Mack even accompanied Laura to the orthodontist when she got her braces put on—the two reportedly filled the dentist's rubber gloves with water and sprayed each other. Mack also took a trip with the Bundys to Laura's grandparents in Lexington, Kentucky. On Valentine's Day, he sent her a dozen red roses!

Chapter 9:

What It's Really Like
To Be So Famous

Because of *Home Alone*, there are very few people in the USA who don't know who Macaulay Culkin is. Some may not know his real name, but even toddlers can recognize the blond boy who smashed his cheeks with his hands and screamed "Ahhh!" in the famous scene. It is fair to say that right now, Mack is the hottest and best known child actor in America. As Mack has learned first hand, there are ups and downs to being in that position.

Happy-go-lucky Mack finds the bright side easily. He gets to ride in fancy limousines and meet other big stars. Mack has been to the White House, where he shook hands with President and Mrs. Bush.

Mack's met Arnold Schwarzenegger and

Mack works out!

Bob Hope. He even got to be the host of *Saturday Night Live,* which was more fun than work. His friends thought that was very cool.

According to Mack, being famous means that he can get the latest Nintendo games before they're out in the stores (the company sends them to him) which is a very big advantage. He likes being able to travel, too. Disneyland, Bermuda, and California are his favorite vacation spots.

Best of all, perhaps, is his friendship with Michael Jackson. Mack is flattered that the usually shy superstar has taken him into his confidence. Mack also realizes that if **he** weren't so famous himself, Michael probably wouldn't have gotten to know him. Michael joined the Culkin clan on their Bermuda holiday last year, and then went to Disneyland with the family. That's where Michael and Mack found out how much they had in common—both are fun-loving pranksters, who enjoyed nothing more than squirting each other with water guns.

Michael invited the Culkins to his multi-acre spread in California, called Neverland. Since he invites very few people into his home, Mack felt especially honored. When he and Michael went out shopping, both donned disguises. Mack wore sunglasses and a hat, Michael put on a phony nose and funny teeth. They both got a kick out of fooling folks.

It was certainly a thrill for Mack when

Michael asked him to be in the "Black or White" video, and, of course, Mack was sensational in it.

In what was perhaps the greatest compliment of all, Michael asked Mack to be part of the singer's exciting new *Dangerous* (named for his latest album) world tour. While Michael, of course, would handle most of the singing and dancing, Mack would come out at a specific spot in the show to dance with Michael.

The prospect is thrilling even though Mack isn't sure if he can do it. The *Dangerous* tour is scheduled to start by the end of 1992 and Mack wants to be part of it. But those kinds of big decisions, naturally, are left to his parents. Mack might, after all, be filming a new movie at that time. And certainly, his school work would have to come first. But just in case it does work out, Mack has started taking private dance lessons.

Mack truly appreciates all the wonderful things that have happened to him since *Home Alone* came out, but even protective parents can't completely shield him from the not-so-fun parts of being famous—like fans finding his house and camping out in front. Or the fact that Mack has to change his phone number so often, he once had to call a friend to find out what his number was *this* week. And especially, it's feeling cooped up at home and not being able to do anything about it.

"I'm not allowed to go out by myself," Mack

has moaned. 'So if there's no one to take me places, I have to just stay home.'' The truth is that if Mack did go out by himself, he might cause a riot. He is besieged by fans almost constantly. There are times when his family has had to hire a bodyguard to stay with Mack, which doesn't feel like a normal life at all.

Still, right now that's the reality of Macaulay Culkin's life. Which, when all is said and done, Mack wouldn't trade with anybody, for anything.

"Oh, no! It's alive!"

Chapter 10:

What's Up Next?

Mack loves making movies and is pretty sure he'll always be an actor. His parents have told him that he can quit anytime he wants to, but right now, that's the furthest thing from his mind. He's looking forward to starring in many more films, and Mack's fans are looking forward to exactly the same thing.

Although Mack will probably sign on for more *Home Alone* sequels, there are other kinds of films on the drawing board. Fans should know that Mack won't always be playing such a good guy!

There's a reason for that. Mack's dad, Kit is looking out for his future. He wants fans to see that Mack is talented enough to play all sorts of roles. As he said recently, "The best thing that can happen to Mack is for him to have the opportunity to be thought of as an actor, not just a cute kid."

In fact, Mack's next film after *Home Alone 2: Lost In New York,* will give him the opportunity to really strut his acting stuff. Mack is cast completely against type, as a very troubled character. The movie is called *The Good Son.* It is about a young boy who goes to live with relatives and slowly discovers that his cousin isn't nearly as nice as he seems on the outside. In fact, the boy is quite evil. Mack has landed the key role of the bad cousin. *The Good Son* will be in theaters in 1993.

Of course, all Mack's new roles won't be dark and serious. He's thinking about playing the lead in a movie based on the comic book character Richie Rich, described as, "a nice kid who's also the world's richest little boy."

A definite in Mack's future is the deal he signed to be in commercials for Sprite soda. He will make two 30-second commercials which will air on TV. "I like the Sprite in you," is the slogan, but privately, the ever-honest Mack has admitted, "I'm not that crazy about the stuff."

As he turns 12 years old, Macaulay Culkin has it all—a loving family, a fabulous career and a bright future—and he knows it.

America's hottest kid is also America's most grateful kid.

Chapter 11:

Mack's Mini-Fact File

Real Name: Macaulay Culkin
Birthday: August 26, 1980
Height: 4′ 4-½″
Weight: 70 lbs.
Hair: Blond
Eyes: Blue
Born & Raised: New York City
Mom & Dad: Patricia (Pat) and Christopher (Kit)
Brothers: Shane, Kieran, Christopher, and Rory
Sisters: Dakota and Quinn
School: Professional Children's School
Grade: Seventh, as of September, 1992
Favorites:
    Food: Hot dogs, salads, popcorn
    Music: Hard rock

Macaulay Culkin is a People's Choice favorite!

Holiday: Halloween
Color: Black
Sport: Dodge ball, skateboarding, bike riding
Animal: Polar bears
Collects: Coins
Place: California
Ice Cream: Vanilla with chocolate syrup on it
Address: Macaulay Culkin, c/o ICM, 40 W. 57th St., New York, NY 10019, or c/o *Home Alone 2: Lost In New York,* 20th Century Fox Films, P.O. Box 900, Beverly Hills, CA 90210.

Mack with Brooke Shields at a Toys for Tots Benefit.

Chapter 12:

The Home Alone Trivia Quiz

How much do you really know about the world's most popular comedy? Take the *Home Alone* Trivia Quiz and find out. The answers are at the end, but don't peek until you're done.

1. **How did Kevin recognize the robber?**
   A. He had three fingers
   B. He had a wart on his forehead
   C. He had a gold tooth
2. **Where did Kevin's family go on vacation?**
   A. London
   B. Paris
   C. New York

Macaulay Culkin hams it up for the paparazzi.

3. **What kind of animal did Buzz (Kevin's brother) have for a pet?**
   A. A tarantula
   B. A snake
   C. A hermit crab
4. **What part of his body did the robber catch on fire?**
   A. His hand
   B. His head
   C. His hand *and* his head
5. **What did the other robber do to his foot?**
   A. He stepped on a nail
   B. He stepped in tar
   C. he stepped on a nail *and* in tar
6. **How did Kevin's mom finally get home?**
   A. In a van
   B. On a plane
   C. In a rental car
7. **What kind of pizza does Kevin like?**
   A. Pepperoni
   B. Plain
   C. Meatball
8. **Who was Kevin most afraid of?**
   A. The robbers
   B. The boogie man
   C. His neighbor
9. **What did Kevin shoplift?**
   A. A watch
   B. A candy bar
   C. A toothbrush

10. **Where did Kevin go before the robbers came?**
    A. Church
    B. The zoo
    C. The supermarket
11. **During which holiday does the movie take place?**
    A. The Fourth of July
    B. Christmas
    C. Thanksgiving
12. **What was Kevin's last name?**
    A. McKenzie
    B. McCallister
    C. McCabe
13. **When Kevin woke up and found himself alone, what did he say?**
    A. "I made my family disappear!"
    B. "Wonder where everyone is?"
    C. "I bet they're playing a joke on me."
14. **What brand of aftershave made him go "Ahhh!"?**
    A. Old Spice
    B. Aqua Velva
    C. Brut

Answers:
1) C; 2) B; 3) A; 4) C; 5) C; 6) A; 7) B; 8) C; 9) C;
10) A; 11) B; 12) B; 13) A; 14) C.

Chapter 13:

Extra! Extra!
The Five Most-Asked
Mack Questions . . .

1. **Where did the name Macaulay come from?**

   "I don't know," says Mack, "you'll have to ask my parents." Mack's dad, in fact, named him after the English historian, Thomas Babbington Macaulay.

2. **I've seen his nickname spelled as Mac and Mack—which is correct?**

   The small superstar prefers it spelled with a K, Mack.

3. **What does he really do when he's home alone?**

   He's never been home alone.

4. **How much money does he have?**

   More than he can count. Safe to say Mack's a multi-millionaire.

Mack wearing his favorite color.